# ABOUT THIS NO NONSENSE
## SUCCESS GUIDE™

This No Nonsense Success Guide, like each Success Guide, has been designed to live up to *both* parts of its name . . . to provide you with useful No Nonsense information *and* to increase your personal chances for Success!

Consulting is one of today's most rewarding self-employment opportunities.

It is a high-income, low-risk business which can bring you great success. GETTING INTO THE CONSULTING BUSINESS provides you with the basic information you need to start your own part-time or full-time consulting business.

You will discover how to start your consulting business, how to write winning proposals and how to set your fees.

The U.S. Government is the world's largest buyer of consulting services — but few consultants know how to do business with Uncle Sam. This book solves that problem.

An Exclusive Special Section features FOUR SEPARATE AND COMPLETE U.S. GOVERNMENT CONSULTING OPPORTUNITIES DIRECTORIES — including Names, Addresses and Telephone Numbers!

This is the one book you need if you are thinking of becoming a consultant now or in the future.

# THE NO NONSENSE LIBRARY

## NO NONSENSE SUCCESS GUIDES

Getting Into the Consulting Business
Getting Into the Mail Order Business
How to Own and Operate a Franchise
How to Run a Business Out of Your Home
How (and Where) to Get the Money to Get Started
The Self-Employment Test

## OTHER NO NONSENSE GUIDES

CAR GUIDES
CAREER GUIDES
COOKING GUIDES
FINANCIAL GUIDES
HEALTH GUIDES
LEGAL GUIDES
PARENTING GUIDES
PHOTOGRAPHY GUIDES
REAL ESTATE GUIDES
STUDY GUIDES
WINE GUIDES

# NO NONSENSE

## SUCCESS GUIDE™

# GETTING INTO THE CONSULTING BUSINESS

## STEVE KAHN

LONGMEADOW PRESS

Getting Into The Consulting Business

Copyright © 1987 by The Keasy Corporation. All rights reserved.

Cover design by Tom Fowler, Inc.

Composition by Tod Clonan Associates, Inc.

Published by Longmeadow Press, 201 High Ridge Road, Stamford, Connecticut 06904. No part of this book may be reproduced or used in any form or by any means, electronic or mechanical, including photocopying, recording, or by an information storage and retrieval system, without permission in writing from the publisher.

No Nonsense Success Guide is a Trade Mark controlled by Longmeadow Press.

ISBN: 0-681-40129-X

Printed in the United States of America

0   9   8   7   6   5   4

# TABLE OF CONTENTS

# 1

# CONSULTING: AN ENTREPRENEUR'S WORKING DEFINITION

In today's competitive and challenging economy, business values these five virtues perhaps above all others:

(1) **Information**
(2) **Efficiency**
(3) **Productivity**
(4) **Objectivity**
(5) **Innovation**

If one were asked to define the basic services which most consultants provide, it would be a virtual duplicate of this list!

*Thus, it is no surprise that consulting is one of today's most consistently exciting and rewarding self-employment opportunities.*

## If Doctors, Lawyers and Accountants Are Professionals, What Is A Consultant?

Consulting has had to overcome a long-standing problem of an uncertain self-image.

Some cynics once considered consulting a form of unemployment. ("Is Tom still looking for a job?" "No, he's become a consultant.")

Others defined consulting as a comedian once did: "A consultant is someone who borrows your watch to tell you what time it is."

By these examples, Rodney Dangerfield would have been the ideal consultant — expecting no respect from his audience.

Today, however, consultants are no longer the object of anyone's mis-directed or mis-guided "humor."

This transformation hasn't come about as the result of a clever advertising or public relations campaign. Rather, it is the product of a business world which has come to appreciate and understand that consultants provide a broad range of fundamental and useful services which they can deliver more productively and more efficiently than anyone else.

Doctors, lawyers and acccountants are, in fact, consultants. If you have a medical problem, you call upon a doctor. If you have a legal problem, you seek out a lawyer. If you have a tax or other accounting problem, you contact an accountant.

We don't consciously think of these professionals as consultants, but that is, in truth, what they are. They bring their skills, experience and education to a problem and then combine that knowledge in an attempt to solve it as ffectively as possible.

*A reliable, respectable consultant provides precisely the same ervice.*

Of course, there are some consultants who produce nferior work. They are no different from the second-rate doctors, lawyers and accountants we have all come across — or, at least, heard about.

To paraphrase a well-known cigarette advertisement, consulting has come a long way.

It is no longer a misunderstood occupation. It is, in fact, a high-profile, high-profit profession which directly meets the needs of today's fast-moving, fast-changing business world.

Consulting fulfills the definition of a profession as established by *The American Heritage Dictionary:* "A body of qualified persons engaged in an occupation of field."

Best of all, it also meets the dictionary's definition of opportunity: "A favorable time or occasion for a certain purpose."

*Thus, if you are thinking of becoming a consultant, your timing and inclination couldn't be better.*

# 2

# WHO CAN BECOME A CONSULTANT?

You can — IF you are ready to deal with the challenge of being self-employed AND if you have experience and expertise in an area which can benefit from the services of independent consultants.

Another book in this *No Nonsense Success Series* — **The Self-Employment Test** — will help you to answer the first item.

Only you can answer the second item, after researching your area of special knowledge and then making an informed judgment about its consulting opportunities and your ability to take advantage of those opportunities.

Chances are that both answers will be affirmative, and that becoming a consultant is an active and attractive option for you.

## A List of Five Diverse and Encouraging Examples

The purpose of this section is to illustrate the virtually limitless consulting opportunities which are available to you, no matter the nature of your present occupation. It is a composite selection of five "ordinary" jobs which were converted into five creative consulting businesses.

### 1. The Traffic Manager

*Employment Background:* As an employee, he was responsible for coordinating the worldwide shipments of his company's products. Consequently, he was thoroughly familiar with shipping rates, shippers and the most inexpensive yet efficient procedures to move merchandise from here to there.

*Consulting Opportunities:* The shipment of merchandise has become an increasingly complicated and competitive process. As a consultant, he knew that most small and mid-size companies did not have the resources to keep track of the constantly changing rules and rates. He quickly established a large and profitable consulting practice by demonstrating that he could help these companies achieve significant shipping savings without having to invest in additional employees or equipment.

### 2. The Party Planner

*Employment Background:* As the promotional coordinator for a public relations agency, she organized parties and other public events for the firm's clients. The functions which she created were always unique, creative and successful.

*Consulting Opportunities:* As a consultant, she could offer her expertise without "any strings attached." When she had been with the PR agency, only clients of the firm (who paid considerable fees for a complete package of services) could seek her counsel. Now, her party-planning skills were available independently. It did not take her long to build an enjoyable consulting business for fees which comfortably exceeded her former salary.

### 3. The Franchise Owner

*Employment Background:* He started several franchise operations, usually with new franchisors whom he considered reputable. He enjoyed the building process more than day-in, day-out management and therefore sold each of his businesses soon after they were successfully established.

*Consulting Opportunities:* As an operating franchisee, he had gained a great deal of "hands-on" experience evaluating franchisors. He had also come to know many franchisees who had before the victims of their own poor judgment. His good reputation and sound judgment was known to the local community of bankers, lawyers and accountants, many of whom directed prospective franchisees to him. He enjoyed advising and protecting his clients. He enjoyed it so much, in fact, that consulting was the first business which he built without any intention of ever selling it.

### 4. The Jewelry Buyer

*Employment Background:* As the merchandise buyer for the largest jewelry store in a regional mall, she developed a reputation as someone whose buying instincts were uncannily on-target. The merchandise which she put on sale was always "hot" and ahead of the competition.

*Consulting Opportunities:* Many smaller, independent retail shops in her area sold jewelry but did not have the contacts or instincts which she had developed. Thus, their jewelry did not "move" as quickly and profitably as possible. She became the jewelry buying consultant to a group of these stores, none of which directly competed with one another. In addition to her consulting fees, she received a small percentage of each client's increased profits — together with a strong sense of satisfaction at being able to exceed her previous level of success.

## 5. The Fireman

*Employment Background:* He was a dedicated, intelligent full-time fireman for 20 years. He had seen too many people killed and injured and too much property needlessly destroyed. Thus, when he could retire on a full pension after 20 years, he took advantage of the opportunity.

*Consulting Opportunities:* You might consider this fireman the least likely candidate for consultancy, but he is included because he is representative of the truth that virtually every occupation has consulting possibilities. In the case of the fireman, he became a fire prevention consultant. In time, his consulting practice became so large that he was able to hire some of his former colleagues in the department when they retired. He was doing what he had always done — saving lives and property — but he was doing it on his own time (no more midnight shifts) and at an increased level of compensation.

Have you noticed the common thread among our examples, as well as among consultants generally? It is this: They genuinely enjoy their work (because they know that they are providing a useful service) and they typically are well-paid for their work (because their commitment produces excellence, which is always deserving of a premium). Together, this combination produces great satisfaction for most successful consultants.

It is perhaps the best reason of all for taking heart from the answer to the question which serves as the title for this chapter.

*The Question: Who can become a consultant?*
*The Answer: You can!*

# 3
# DETERMINING YOUR CONSULTING SKILLS

All consultants, whether they are computer wizards or franchising experts, share the need to develop five primary skills.

In advance of making the decision to become a consultant, you have an obligation to honestly determine your personal level of skill within each category. Weakness in a particular category should not deter your decision to become a consultant, but it should perhaps delay it until you have increased your confidence and competence in the area of uncertainty.

## Primary Consulting Skill No. 1:
### The Ability to Analyze

Most often, consultants are hired to solve a particular problem.

Thus, the ability to analyze a complex set of circumstances

and information becomes a primary consulting skill.

You will have to have the ability to carefully listen, then comprehend the nature of the challenge, and ultimately break it down into components which will enable you to solve the entire problem.

Analysis is a skill which requires patience and persistence. As a consultant, you will have to manifest such patience and persistence in order to become recognized as a skillful problem-solver.

If it were an "easy" problem, the client wouldn't need you in the first place!

## Primary Consulting Skill No. 2:
## The Ability To Organize

Your analysis will, of course, require some organization.

The greater need for organization will come (a) as you work through the problem and (b) you begin to develop the solutions.

Perhaps the greatest benefits of organization are these: You will have complete control over the problem-solving process and you will be so organized that, at a moment's notice, you can give your client a current status report without disrupting your work flow.

Clients *love* consultants who can provide them with information upon demand.

## Primary Consulting Skill No. 3:
## The Ability To Speak Clearly

Within the analysis category, we observed that you will have to listen carefully so that you can fully appreciate your client's needs. You will also have to develop the ability to speak clearly.

You will have to speak clearly so that your questions can be understood; more importantly, you will have to speak clearly so that your answers can be understood.

Many clients will ask for verbal as well as written presentations — and you will have to develop the ability to provide them in either mode.

## Primary Consulting Skill No. 4: The Ability To Write Clearly

The end product of most consultants' work will be some form of written report.

Long after your assignment has ended, that report will be the evidence of your consulting abilities. It is, in many ways, your ultimate "calling card."

Thus, your product — your written presentation — will have to be as good as you can make it. If you are comfortable with the three previous skill categories — analyzing, organizing and speaking — but have some discomfort about writing, don't even think about going to the consulting business until you have improved your writing abilities to a higher level of confidence.

## Primary Consulting Skill No. 5: Marketing Your Consulting Business

There's a strong argument that this should really be listed as the first skill — because if your consulting practice doesn't obtain clients, you won't have anyone taking advantage of your other skills.

The reason we have positioned marketing here is that we will be devoting an entire chapter to the marketing of your consulting business. However, it is such an important factor that any list of primary consulting skills would be incomplete and invalid without its inclusion.

# 4

# THE ADVANTAGES OF CONSULTING

Every self-employment opportunity is blessed with advantages and burdened with disadvantages. Some of the advantages of consulting are especially attractive.

## A Virtually Economy-Proof Business

When the economy is slow, and businesses are especially worried about keeping their costs in check, they turn to consultants in place of hiring additional personnel. They can easily control their consulting costs without adding any permanent payroll expense.

When the economy is booming, and businesses are taking on new business (and problems) faster than anticipated, they turn to consultants because of the increased workload.

Thus, in good times and bad, consulting is an on-demand service for which there is always a demand.

## Consultants Are Truly Independent

In a business sense, a consultant's independence is one of his most valuable virtues. It enables him to bring objective, unbiased perspective to a problem.

In a personal sense, a consultant's independence can enable him to maintain a very flexible lifestyle.

Many consultants work at home (a subject which is covered in **How To Run A Business Out Of Your Home**, another in this series of *No Nonsense Success Guides*). Thus — except for those times when he has a scheduled appointment or other timely commitment — he can establish his own flexible schedule.

Unlike a shopkeeper, a consultant doesn't have an "opening" business hour.

If he's a night owl, he can work all night.

If she's an early bird, she can begin working before the sun rises.

Whether the consultant is billing by the hour, the day or the assignment, he has to make certain to deliver an honest day's work for his consulting fee.

The advantage is that he can determine when his day begins and ends.

## Consulting Can Be Started As A Part-Time Business

If your consulting work does not come into conflict with your obligations as an employee, it is possible for you to begin consulting on a part-time basis.

This approach obviously has several advantages.

You will still have a steady income, and you will have the opportunity to evaluate yourself as a consultant without jeopardizing your security.

You will also discover whether being self-employed is a comfortable experience for you. Even a part-time consulting business requires full-time management skills, and you will be able to determine your taste (or distaste) for that aspect of self-employment.

## Consulting Requires A Small Investment

Consulting does not require any significant expenses for equipment.

You will need an office-quality typewriter, business stationery, and perhaps a copier and a computer, depending on the nature of your consulting business. On the other hand, you can purchase only the stationery and rent the typewriter, use a library's copier, and put off acquiring the computer.

If you do not need an office, and can arrange for your existing home telephone to be answered in a business-like manner, your expenses are further reduced.

Thus, especially if you enter consulting on a part-time basis, it can be accomplished with a very low level of direct financial risk.

## Consulting Is Constantly Changing, Continually Challenging

Even if your consulting business lies within a relatively narrow specialty, you will be faced with constant changes and challenges. You never know what the next call, the next assignment, will bring.

This diversity is exciting and exhilirating, and adds an edge of enjoyment (as well as unpredictability) to a consulting practice.

Nothing, not even consulting, is perfect. The following chapter presents some of consulting's disadvantages.

# 5

# THE DISADVANTAGES OF CONSULTING

On balance, the advantages of becoming a consultant appear to outweigh the disadvantages. However, there are some significant disadvantages which you will have to consider in advance of starting a consulting business.

## You Will Be Competing With Many Large Consulting Firms

As consulting has grown as a self-employment option for individuals, it has also grown as an attractive profit center for larger organizations. There have always been straight-forward consulting firms, but now accounting firms are entering the consulting business very aggressively as are investment banking firms, insurance companies and even manufacturing and service companies (who have discovered a new way to make profitable use of their in-house skills and employees).

As in many David vs. Goliath confrontations, David can often win through sheer imagination and courage. In the business sense, that translates to a commitment of personal service, quick response time and an understanding that the prospective client must be sold on the premise that he can only gain by doing business with the independent consultant rather than the larger firm.

It is a strategy which can succeed, but it is a circumstance that will put added marketing pressure on your consulting practice.

## You Will Be Competing With Many Small Consulting Firms

An attractive self-employment opportunity does not go unnoticed, so you will have much more competition in general.

These small, one-person consulting firms pose a different marketing challenge.

They may simply try to edge you out by sharply reducing their consulting fees.

You have to be careful not to underprice your consulting services. You can often successfully overcome this tactic by pointing out the relationship between price and performance ("you get what you pay for") and that, even though you would very much like the assignment, you would be short-changing both yourself and the client. You might not gain a consulting assignment immediately but most prospective clients will be impressed by your self-confidence and sense of self-worth and they will keep that in mind the next time they have a consulting assignment.

## Isolation

Most consultants work alone. If you are used to the bustle and personal interchange of an office or plant environment, you may become uncomfortable within the isolation of a one-person consulting practice.

Most consultants adjust, by making certain that they have many opportunities to speak with and see other people. Some consultants do not. If you are in the latter category, the sooner you make that self-discovery, the happier you will be.

## Motivation

Working alone, perhaps even at home, is always a difficult situation.

Who's going to know if you oversleep or put off your checklist of things to do until tomorrow?

You are, of course, and only you will suffer from the failure to discipline yourself.

You must be motivated to approach each day as a full, demanding work day — even if you don't have any clients yet. You certainly won't acquire them by oversleeping or procrastinating!

Lack of self-discipline can become a serious problem, one which you have to be aware of and correct at its first appearance.

## Travel

Often a consulting assignment may require some travel, to a distant plant or a branch office.

If traveling is not something which you enjoy doing, be certain that you carefully considered the possible travel demands of your particular consulting business.

It is possible that such demands will be infrequent, if at all; on the other hand, if travel is a high probability, you may have to review and/or reconsider your decision to become a consultant.

## Getting Paid

This disadvantage may surprise you, but, when a company's cash flow is tight, a consultant's fee is often the first due bill which it puts on "hold."

Consulting fees are typically apportioned over the life of the assignment. A typical arrangement might be one-third of the fee when the assignment begins, one-third when it is half-completed, the final third upon completion.

It is that last portion which, under certain circumstances, can be in jeopardy: You've done the work, the client has it in hand, and he will suffer no loss or damage by delaying his final payment to you.

Thus, it is in your self-interest to carefully check out a prospective client's business reputation and credit rating. His reputation can usually be ascertained by word of mouth within the business community; his credit rating can be purchased from a reputable credit-reporting service for a relatively modest fee. It is an inexpensive "insurance policy" which can spare you considerable grief and aggravation upon the completion of a consulting assignment.

# 6

# HOW SHOULD YOU POSITION YOUR CONSULTING BUSINESS?

There are essentially two categories of consultants: Broad-based general consultants who proclaim themselves able to deal with virtually any problem or project that arises within the everyday business environment, and specialized consultants, like "consulting engineers," who only accept assignments which fall within their more narrowly defined area of expertise.

It is very difficult for an individual consultant to market himself as a general consultant.

Step back a moment and think of this: Imagine you are faced with a complicated legal tax problem, and you have been given the names of three lawyers or law firms.

The first lawyer is a single practitioner. He does everything. He writes wills, drafts corporate resolutions and even handles some criminal matters. He has a copy of the Internal Revenue Service Code in his office and tells you that he is confidently prepared to handle your problem.

The second name is that of a large law firm, which is divided into departments which represent virtually every aspect of the law. It has a reputable tax department, and you have met with one of the tax partners, who has assured you that your matter can be handled within his department. He has several associates with experience in related matters and he will put one of them on your case as soon as you give him the go-ahead. Of course, he will keep an eye on the case and supervise his associate's work on your behalf.

The third person on the list is a lawyer who specializes in tax law. Like the first attorney, he is a single practitioner; unlike the first attorney, he limits his practice to tax-related matters. Although he is obviously busy and successful — the phone never stops ringing and his desk is covered with case files — he is willing to carefully listen to your problem. If he takes your case, he will handle it personally, except for some technical research matters which he will assign to a paralegal employee. He admits that your matter is complicated, but he reassures you that he is confident that it can be resolved in your favor. It may take considerable time (his) and money (yours), but he offers you a high level of confidence and competence.

Which of the three lawyers are you going to hire?

The first lawyer is out of the running. He is no doubt competent, but the complexity of your tax problem is really beyond the scope of his everyday practice.

The law firm is a possibility. It is reputable, successful and long-established. However, you're somewhat uncomfortable about being handled as just another case within the tax department. The tax partner you met was courteous and competent, but he did imply that you would not take high priority within his busy department.

The third lawyer, the tax specialist, is a good friend of the tax partner at the firm we just reviewed — and, in fact, has occasionally lost clients to it. The reason for that attrition is that these clients wanted a "full-service" tax counsel, confident that someone would always be there to handle questions. The tax lawyer could not offer that certainty; when he was in a trial or on vacation, he was simply out of reach.

Nevertheless, you would probably select the third lawyer, the tax specialist. You would not mind giving up the security blanket of a "full-service" law firm in exchange for the "hands-on" involvement of a committed attorney with enormous experience in your specific area of need.

*Similarly, an individual consultant who specializes in one area is more likely to succeed than one who proffers to solve a wide variety of problems.*

*However, within this area of specialization, he should offer as many consulting services as he can reasonably manage.*

Thus, for example, if you are a computer programming consultant, you should offer more than the ability to custom-design computer programs for clients. You should also offer to set up in-company training programs; create operating manuals; help the client market the programs which you created to *his* clients; and generally provide a broad range of creative and support services in addition to your basic computer-programming design consultancy.

Such an approach will enhance your credibility as a specialist while enabling you to accept additional assignments which might otherwise be given to a larger firm.

Thus, in most instances, the individual consultant should establish himself as a specialist. Within that speciality, he should position himself to provide as many *related* consulting services as he can comfortably deliver.

If that balance can be achieved, the consultant will have created "the best of all possible (consulting) worlds."

# CONSULTING FOR BUSINESS

Companies hire consultants for four primary reasons.

## 1. Consultants Can Be Hired As Needed

As a general rule, employers are keeping their number of permanent full-time employees as low as possible. That is why, for example, the office temporary service business is booming.

Consultants are beneficiaries of the same principle. As the need arises, more and more companies are electing to hire (temporary) consultants rather than (permanent) employees.

## 2. Consultants Can Help Meet Deadlines

A computer company may be introducing several new models simultaneously. It has announced a firm introduction date, but it still needs technical manuals for two of the models.

This is an example of an ideal consulting opportunity: Helping a client to achieve its objectives on time.

### 3. Consultants Provide Objectivity

One of a consultant's most valuable virtues is his impartiality. Ideally, he approaches an assignment without any bias, studies it with a complete sense of open-mindedness and then delivers a solution free of any subjective factors.

A company's employees are often too close to the problem or project in question. The consultant can approach it from a distance. His solution may be similar or identical to the employees', but even that outcome will reassure the client company because it will have been provided by a completely objective source.

### 4. Consultants Can Override "Company Politics"

Companies are frequently burdened with opposing political factions, in-fighting between departments and similar internal corporate strife.

In such cases, the consultant virtually serves as a referee brought in to settle the fight.

Such an assignment can easily become uncomfortable for the consultant, who will be resented as an "outsider" by *all* sides.

Such discomfort notwithstanding, this is a common circumstance leading to the decision to hire a consultant.

The good news for prospective consultants is that none of these primary reasons appear to be temporary. Each appears to be a permanent component of the way corporate America does business. If that is true (and we believe that it is), then consulting for business should continue to be a promising and prosperous profession.

# 8

# CONSULTING FOR INDIVIDUALS

Until recently, consultants expected to be hired by two major client groups: Business (the subject of the preceeding chapter) and Government (the subject of the succeeding chapter).

Individuals were not even regarded as marginal prospects for a consultant's services. That has changed and the very subject of this chapter — *Consulting for Individuals* — has become consulting's newest phenomenon.

The fundamental reasons that individuals have become consulting clients is because they have *more* money and *less* time.

Two-paycheck families are increasingly common, particularly in households where there are either no children or the children have grown up. These families have considerable sums of money available and typically employ consultants to improve the quality of their lives.

One of the negative consequences of busy, hard-working, two-income families is that they have less and less time to spend with one another. These families employ consultants to improve the quality of their time.

Many consultants — such as interior designers and financial planners — can easily transfer their skills from business and government to individuals. They may adjust their fees and the magnitude of their services but they can comfortably accommodate individual clients.

On the other hand, entirely new consultant categories have been created by this new market of individual clients. Individuals can now hire such providers as personal shoppers and personal fitness trainers (who make house calls).

Certain professional consulting practices will be able to take advantage of this new marketplace.

A computer consultant, for example, can easily supply an individual with a breakdown of the best computers and computer programs available for his particular needs. A consultant who specializes in corporate time management can also help an over-worked, stressed-out executive manage his personal time more efficiently.

As more and more individuals discover the usefulness of consultants, consultants in many areas will become beneficiaries of consulting's newest client category: Individuals.

# CHAPTER

# 9

# CONSULTING FOR GOVERNMENT

*The U.S. Government is the biggest buyer of goods and services in the world.*

Yet many producers of goods and services — including consultants — are (1) unaware of this dramatic fact and (2) actively afraid of doing business with the Federal Government because it threatens to become a complicated and cumbersome and even intimidating process.

There is still considerable truth to the second point, but the greater truth is that the Federal Government is filled with immense opportunities for consultants (as well as other small businesses).

The Government's primary purchasing agent, the General Services Administration (GSA), solicits small businesses, including consultants, with this open invitation:

**Regardless of size, firms seeking to expand their operations and profits should consider doing business with the U.S. Government.**

Opportunities are plentiful because this consumer buys more goods and services than any other customer in the free enterprise system. And everyone has a potential share since the Government's needs vary in size from those which can be met by small, singly owned enterprises to those requiring the resources of large, corporately held companies.

Of course, it requires sound information and skill to take advantage of these opportunities.

In general, a firm must know where in the Federal structure to market its products, how to make itself and its products known, how and where to obtain the necessary forms and papers, and how to bid for the opportunity to sell specific goods or services.

## How The Government Buys

Federal purchasing agencies buy goods and services in two ways: by advertising for bids and by negotiation.

**Advertising for Bids.** Every Government purchasing agency maintains a so-called "bidders list." Each of these lists consists of those manufacturing and service companies (such as consultants) which have informed the specific purchasing office that they are ready, willing and able to provide that agency with the products or services which they sell.

To be placed on a "bidders list," a consultant has to request the necessary forms from those Federal agencies which he considers to be prospective clients.

There are two important considerations to keep in mind with respect to being included on those bidders lists:

*(1) There is no single "master list." You will have to make separate applications for each specific agency's list.*

*(2) You will not be added to any Federal agency's list unless and until you request to be added on — and until you have completed the proper Government forms required by that particular agency's purchasing office.*

A strong starting point for finding those Federal agencies which buy consulting services can be found in the first section of our four-part *Government Consulting Opportunities Directories*, which begins on page 75.

Beyond that, consultants interested in working for the Government should consider subscribing to the "Commerce Business Daily," which is published Mondays through Fridays by the U.S. Department of Commerce.

This publication includes a daily list of U.S. Government procurement invitations for bids as well as a great deal of additional information which can help the anxious consultant navigate his way through the Federal purchasing process.

As of this writing, an annual subscription to the "Commerce Business Daily" is $88.00 by 2nd class mail or $160.00 via first class mail.

It can be ordered from the Superintendent of Documents, Government Printing Office, Washington, DC 20402. Payment must accompany your order.

Usually, when a contract is advertised for bid, it will be awarded to a winning bidder — based on his price, the specifics of his bid and his ability to perform. *However,*

Government purchasing officers do have the authority to reject all bids received when they believe that such a decision is in the best interests of the Government.

The Government's purchasing alternative to advertising for bids is buying by negotiation.

**Buying by Negotiation.** Under certain circumstances, which are prescribed by law and applicable regulations, Government purchases may be made by negotiation with qualified suppliers, and without formal advertising for bids.

In purchasing by negotiation, the procurement office also makes use of its bidders list for the particular item or service. Here the office asks for price quotations or proposals, including detailed analyses of estimated costs or other evidence of reasonable prices. These "requests for proposals" are sent to a number of suppliers so that the purchase will be made on a competitive basis.

After reviewing the various quotations received on a proposed purchase, the contracting officer frequently will negotiate further with the suppliers who have submitted acceptable proposals, seeking the most advantageous contract for the Government.

We acknowledged at the outset that doing business with the Federal Government is still cumbersome, but it can be a profitable source of business for consultants as well as a prestigious one.

If you can list Federal Government agencies as consulting clients, you will have added significant credibility to your status.

There are, in fact, at least 35 major Federal civilian purchasing offices which specifically list "consultant services" on their buying schedule. You will find the names and addresses of each of these procurement offices beginning on page 77.

The Federal Government is not the only level of government which hires consultants. State, county and city agencies have frequent use for consultants, as well. You will have to do some local research to locate the contacts you will need to solicit and obtain assignments from these non-Federal agencies.

On every level, Government agencies offer consultants significant business opportunities.

# 10

# THE LEGAL ASPECTS OF CONSULTING

The new consultant will have to deal with all of the legal details which are required in any new business plus one consideration which is somewhat unique to the consulting business (at least in contrast to other professional practices).

## Selecting Your Form of Business Organization

You have three choices of business organization. Each has its advantags and disadvantages.

**1. Sole proprietorship.** This is the least costly and least complicated way of starting a business. A sole proprietorship can be organized almost instantly, so long as you meet local regulations (which we'll discuss later in this chapter).

Among its disadvantages are that you have unlimited personal liability with respect to the financial and legal obligations of the business and that (as the name suggests) the business will be entirely dependent on your good health and your good ideas for its growth and survival.

Nevertheless, because of its simplicity and directness, it is probably the most popular method of organizing a new business by an individual entrepreneur.

**2. Partnership.** If you will be joined in the founding of your business by one or more co-entrepreneurs, then forming a partnership is a possible form of organization for your venture. Legal fees for creating a partnership are usually more costly than those for creating a sole proprietorship but less costly than those for creating a corporation.

Among the disadvantages of a partnership are that it can be difficult to get rid of a bad partner; each general partner is bound by the decisions (and financial obligations) of every other general partner; and the death, withdrawal or bankruptcy of a partner can endanger the survival of the entire business.

Among its advantages are the additional capital a partner (or partners) can provide and the old adage that "two heads are better than one."

**3. Corporation.** Organizing a corporation is the most complicated and most costly of the three options. The greatest advantage of the corporate form of business organization is that its shareholders (its owners) have limited liability for the obligations of the firm.

However, the on-going accounting, legal and tax-reporting obligations of a corporation are considerably more demanding (and expensive and time-consuming) than those of a sole proprietorship or partnership.

There is a category of corporation which combines the protective feature of the traditional corporation (limited liability to its shareholders) while permitting the income (and losses) of the business to flow to you individually as if the corporation were a partnership or sole proprietorship.

This category of corporation is called the subchapter S corporation. A "Sub-S" corporation, as it's typically called, must meet certain legal requirements as established by the Internal Revenue Service. Consult your attorney and accountant at the time you are organizing your business; they can advise you as to the possible benefits or disadvantages of this category or corporation as applied to your personal circumstances.

## Meeting Regulations

When beginning a consulting business, you will have to be in compliance with all applicable state, local and Federal regulations.

These will include such diverse details as making certain that your business location is properly zoned for your enterprise; filing a fictitious name certificate with the proper authorities (typically the County Clerk) if you are conducting your business under a name other than your own; and acquiring the necessary tax and sales tax identification numbers and authorizations from your state's tax and revenue authorities.

An experienced local attorney, one who has other small businesses as clients, will be able to provide you with a useful checklist of the regulations which you will have to meet when you are in the process of organizing your business. There are more than you might have imagined but, despite their number, they are typically simple and inexpensive to fulfill.

## Consulting Contracts: Do You Need One Or Not?

Professionals such as doctors and lawyers perform their services and then bill for them in the ordinary course of business. A contract between the parties — even if they are relative strangers to one another — is highly unusual under these circumstances.

Many consultants feel the same way about contracts. They do not believe in them and do not employ them in the conduct of their consulting business.

Many others, having been burned by illegal or at least immoral client behavior (see *Getting Paid* in Chapter 5), would not undertake a consulting assignment without first executing a contract.

Our view is that no client should object to a simple, straightforward letter of agreement. This arrangement is considerably less formal than a full-length contract and can typically be drafted without the assistance of legal counsel. While such a letter will protect the consultant's interests, it will also serve as a definition of the client's needs.

Even the least complicated letter of agreement between a consultant and his client should cover these three basic items:

### 1. Description of Consultant's Services.

This paragraph should clearly outline the consulting

services which are to be performed. Clients tend to have a natural tendancy to unintentionally expand these services during the course of a consulting assignment *(Question A leads to Question B, etc.)*. Upon the mutual consent of both the consultant and the client, this paragraph should provide for the inclusion of additional consulting services which are not anticipated at the beginning of the assignment.

## 2. The Time Frame of The Consulting Assignment.

We know of a consultant who took on a six-months consulting assignment which turned into a three-year project. Since consulting is a business filled with many variables, a definitive stop-and-start schedule is not always realistic.

Where the time frame can be definitively determined, this paragraph becomes a very simple item. Where the time frame has some "open-ended" possibilities, this paragraph should provide for written authorization from the client to continue the assignment at certain predetermined intervals. Alternatively, the initiative can come from the consultant, who can send the client a one-paragraph letter each time the assignment is extended with a request to approve the extension by simply acknowledging the letter.

## 3. A Payment Schedule and The Issue of Expenses.

Some clients like to pay for short-term assignments with one payment, either at the inception or conclusion of the assignment. In that instance, obviously, we would suggest negotiating for the payment at the beginning.

Most consulting arrangements provide for a series of payments, and this paragraph should simply list the schedule of due dates to which both parties have agreed.

The question of expenses can become the subject of

dispute between the client and the consultant. Typically, such ordinary items as a consultant's parking fees or highway tolls (if the assignment is within easy commuting distance) are not defined as expenses to be borne by the client. However, if long-distance travel or similarly costly expenses are involved, they should be defined and payment therefore should be provided for on a timely basis so that the consultant does not suffer any undue discomfort from advancing his own money for such items.

These three matters are the heart of the client/consultant relationship and both the client and the consultant will operate more comfortably within a simple framework which will serve to prevent any misunderstandings between the parties.

# HOW TO MARKET YOUR CONSULTING SERVICES

The marketing of a consulting business can be summarized in one word: **IT.**

I — **Image.**

T — **Target.**

## The Consultant's Image

Every new business is faced with the challenge of establishing a positive image, so that customers will feel safe and secure when they make the decision to do business with the new business.

For a new consulting business, the creation of a positive image is critical. A consultant's clients *must* feel safe and secure when they make the decision to engage his services. It is often the primary catalyst for the selection of one consultant over another.

That image can best be established by two components, one of which can be purchased and one of which (as the saying goes) "money can't buy."

## 1. The Consultant's Reputation.

If you are already well known within your field at the time you begin your consulting practice, you will have a priceless advantage.

Your ex-employer will be sorry to see you go, and your former competitors will be thrilled at the prospect of your potential availability to them now that you are in business for yourself.

This is the marketing aspect of consulting which no sum of money can buy. It also explains why a consultant's first client is often his former employer, who is eager to continue utilizing his valuable skills.

## 2. The Consultant's Targets.

There are three categories of clients which must be reached by a new consultant: Clients already using services similar or identical to his. Clients looking for providers of such services. And, most challenging of all, clients which the consultant has targeted as key prospects — clients who *should* be using his services because they could materially benefit by them.

The categories can be reached by traditional means: A telephone call or a letter of introduction.

In any event, the consultant needs some printed material to announce his presence.

The most effective approach to a simple, professionally-prepared brochure which describes the consulting services which he offers and, just as importantly, modestly but thoroughly establishes his level of credibility and competence.

Since consultants don't usually employ radio or television or newspaper advertising, this brochure will become your marketing linchpin. You should spend a great deal of time and effort to make certain that it represents you as successfully as possible.

The only traditional advertising media which we would suggest for new consultants are trade publications within his field. Many of these publications have "business card" classified sections, which are often literally reprints of the advertiser's own business cards. They are typically included in *each* issue of the publication and, because repetition is one of the ingredients which builds a reputation, frequently result in inquiries which lead to consulting assignments from a surprising range of clients.

## Promotion Is Helpful

Whereas you will have to pay for advertising, promotion will not cost you anything — directly. Indirectly, the cost of promotion will include all of the expenses incurred in reaching those people who can promote you and your service.

These would include editors, columnists, television producers and radio talk show hosts.

If you or your service are sufficiently unique or interesting to warrant coverage by a newspaper, magazine, radio or television station, you will have a distinct marketing advantage.

Studies indicate that consumers regard "editorial" coverage with less skepticism and more enthusiasm than "advertising" material.

Thus, if you can successfully promote yourself and your service, you will have achieved significant credibility while saving considerable advertising expense.

Promotion is a useful marketing medium for a new, start-up consulting business.

## Word-of-Mouth Is Best of All

Satisfied customers are the most valuable asset of any business. If you are able to satisfy your clients, they will build your reputation faster than any carefully planned advertising and promotion program.

# 12

# HOW TO PRICE YOUR CONSULTING SERVICES

This is one of the most difficult questions facing a new consultant.

A portion of the difficulty results from simply not knowing what the prevailing consultant's pay scale "out there" in the "real world" is. And a portion of the difficulty results from the typical fears which all new consultants face: Establishing fees which will not discourage prospective clients from using their services.

*The basic assumption which a consultant must make is that he is entitled to a fair return for his time, knowledge and services.*

A new consultant will also have to factor in an element which he never had to consider as an employee: Indirect expenses. These include everything from rent to insurance premiums to telephone bills to the cost of designing and printing stationery. These are expenses which are already in

lace, whether he has 50 clients or none. And they must be
actored into his fee structure in order to build and maintain
profitable consulting business.

## Consulting Fees Based On Time

Traditionally, consultants have been paid in direct
elationship to the time which they dedicate to a specific
ssignment.

These fees have been established by the hour, by the day,
y the week and by the month.

Many consulting arrangements are still based on this
rrangement — with the daily *(per diem)* fee probably the
most prevalant.

If that is an arrangement you are considering, you are still
aced with the problem of what that fee should be. Determin-
ng that fee will be based on a formula containing three
lements: (1) Your own sense of self-worth. (2) Your client's
ense of your value to him. (3) What the competition is
harging.

It is difficult and not especially helpful to provide finite
onsulting fees in a book which will remain in print over a
eriod of time, during which conditions and circumstances
vill change. A general observation with respect to consulting
ees is that the more unique your consulting services, the
igher your consulting fees.

Thus, an engineer with a very specific and special set of
kills (and, therefore, presumably less direct competition)
an typically charge more than a writer, whose essential
kills are more widely available. In this comparison, we will

use some numbers to illustrate the distinction. Whereas th
writer might be able to charge $250 per day, the enginee
might be able to command a consulting fee of $750 pe
day.

## Consulting Fees Based On The Assignment

Sometimes, the client will have a specific budget for
specific consulting assignment. In these circumstances, h
may ask you to offer a "flat fee" for your services.

Since, as we have already observed, consulting consists o
many variables, this is a difficult pricing approach.

If you cannot avoid this form of compensation (which i
often the case with Government agencies, for example), yo
will have to make certain that you have taken all of th
elements of the assignment into consideration before settin
your fee. Once established, that fee will not be increase
and you will have to live with it even if it proves to b
oppressive.

Thus, our only caution here would be to be very conserva
tive in establishing a fee which cannot be adjusted. If yo
believe that it can be accomplished in 20 hours, build in som
(reasonable) extra time. If you believe your expenses will b
$500, add 15% to your estimate.

Over time, you may be in a position to establish such fee
with much greater confidence. In the beginning, howeve
flat fees can result in a somewhat uncomfortable arrange
ment from the consultant's point of view.

## Consulting Fees Based On Performance

Clients (usually small or start-up businesses) may suggest paying a consultant fees based on the outcome of his work. This is an approach to be avoided even when you are just starting.

The most significant disadvantages of such an arrangement is that you have no control over the results which will determine your ultimate level of compensation.

There is a version of this approach which you can occasionally employ. In this instance, you can offer to work for reasonable but slightly below-average fees together with a "performance bonus" attached. You will run the same risk which we have already noted but you will at least have been paid a minimum fee even if the "performance bonus" never materializes.

It's easy to price a microwave oven or even the cost of drafting a simple will. It is much more difficult to establish consulting fees. Obviously, you will have to do so — and at a level which offers the client fair value and brings you a fair return for your labors. This can be accomplished so long as you are aware of the consultant's greatest pricing mistake: *Underpricing himself.*

Consulting clients are no different than consumers in general: They believe in getting what they pay for.

They are, however, different in one critical aspect: They understand that (confident) consultants don't have close-out sales!

# 13

# THE RECORDS YOU MUST MAINTAIN FOR YOUR CONSULTING BUSINESS

It is well established that the burden of proof to substantiate income and expenses falls on the taxpayer, not the tax collector. Yet, the tax collector — the Internal Revenue Service — has not established *how* these records should be created and maintained. Thus, the burden of proof is yours — and the freedom to organize the most useful record-keeping system you can devise is yours, as well.

## What Your Records Must Be Able To Tell You At A Glance

Your consulting business (every business, in fact) should be able to derive three critical pieces of data from its records at any time:

(1) **How much cash you owe.**
(2) **How much cash you are due,**
(3) **How much cash you have on hand.**

## To Track These Three Facts, You Will Need To Maintain Five Basic Journals

(1) **Check Register:** This should record each check you disburse, the date of the disbursement, the number of the check, to whom it was made out (the payee), the amount of money disbursed, and for what purposed the payment was made.

(2) **Cash Receipts:** This should show the amount of money received, from whom, and for what.

(3) **Sales Journal:** This should record each business transaction, the date of the transaction, for whom it was performed and the amount of the invoice (including sales tax, if applicable).

(4) **Voucher Register:** This is a record of bills, money owed, the date of the bill, to whom it is owed, the amount, and the service performed or the product sold.

(5) **General Journal:** This is a means of adjusting some entries in the other four journals, a record-keeping technique your accountant will explain to you when he helps you to set up your business record-keeping system.

## What Kind of Record-Keeping System Should You Use?

It depends on the nature of your business, and can best be determined after an analysis of your particular business' needs together with your accountant.

Sometimes, a record-keeping system (at least at the beginning) can be incredibly simple, as simple as setting up different envelopes for different purposes: An expense envelope, an income envelope, a bills outstanding envelope, etc. Such a primitive method usually becomes cumbersome, despite its simplicity, and has to be replaced by a less casual system.

Many consultants who own a computer employ one of the many useful (and increasingly inexpensive) computer programs designed to help a business keep track of its income and expenses. These programs can serve many other business purposes, as well, and can give a small business a level of record-keeping sophication which was once only available to large companies.

Finding the best programs — or software — can be a challenging task. You will want to buy programs which can expand as your business activities expand — and ones which will not quickly become obsolete. Because the importance, availability and usefulness of computer software has exploded in recent years, you may find assistance in regard to record-keeping and money-management programs from sources you would not ordinarily consider. Some of the most current, state-of-the-art programs are being developed (and sold) by major accounting firms and local banks.

## Keeping Track of "Hidden" Expenses

Every business suffers from "hidden" expenses which the small business owner often forgets to record — but which can make a considerable difference to your "bottom line."

They are different for each business, but this example will give you a sense of the possibilities.

Every business should make provisions for bounced checks, which are usually returned because of "insufficient funds."

In a service business, such as consulting, you should compare the amount of time you estimated a project would take to the amount of time it actually did take. Time *is* money, especially for the self-employed, and if your estimates are often wrong, you will have a "hidden" expense which will not remain in hiding for long!

It is difficult to make generalities, but it is not difficult to suggest that every business has such pitfalls, such "hidden" expenses, and that keeping track of them — and making adjustments once you have established what they are *really* costing you in time and money — is a record-keeping priority.

## Miscellaneous Records

We are simply going to list three of the records most common to a broad variety of businesses.

### Advertising
In this category, you should include everything from the cost of a Yellow Pages ad to the cost of the phone calls which you made soliciting new business. It is not a bad idea to keep a simultaneous record of what each advertising expenditure produced in new revenue.

### Client Records

Your business is built on satisfied customers, and the more you know about each of them, the better your chances for repeat business. Maintaining current information about your clients will enable you to serve them better and see them more!

### Telephone Record-Checking

The telephone can be insidious. You can find yourself using it when you're not even aware of it!

Not only can misuse of the phone cost you time, it can cost you surprisingly large sums of money. Be sure that you have not been charged for calls or information requests you didn't make, equipment you didn't rent or services which were not provided. Many consultants "log" each of their calls; it is not a bad idea for every consultant to do that occasionally.

## The Benefits of Keeping Good Records

Every business *has* to maintain records, so they might as well carry a number of benefits with them — and these are three of the best benefits which will accrue to you as the product of good record-keeping:

**(1) Your accounting bills will be reduced.** Accountants typically bill for the hours they work on your business. If they can locate the information they need quickly and efficiently, your bills for accounting services can be dramatically lowered.

**(2) You won't worry about the IRS.** The IRS may not tell you how to keep your records, but they certainly expect you o produce complete and accurate records in case they have a question. Good records are a taxpayer's strongest defense.

**(3) You'll sleep better — for two reasons.** The first reason s (2) above, and the second reason is that you will always be confident that your record-keeping system can provide you with the factual, bottom-line information you need to make better — and more profitable — business decisions.

# 14

# HOW TO MAKE YOUR CONSULTING BUSINESS CREDIT-WORTHY

The greatest single reason for business failure is lack of sufficient funding. This book is not designed to help you raise money, but it is designed to help you manage your consulting business — and your business' money.

Therefore, the best advice we can give you is that if you can establish cordial and productive relationships with three groups of people, your money management worries can be significantly reduced. These groups are:

(1) **Your local banks.**
(2) **Your suppliers.**
(3) **Your clients.**

## Your Local Bank

There is some truth to the saying that "banks will only lend you money when you *don't* need it." Thus, it makes sense to introduce yourself to your banker of choice at a time when you don't want anything from him.

Chances are that you already have a personal banking relationship with a bank in your town. If you have been a steady customer, perhaps one who has taken and repaid some loans promptly, then you have an advantage when you are seeking to extend that personal relationship to a business relationship.

A banker familiar with you will most likely welcome you, and give you helpful advice with respect to opening and maintaining a business checking account at his institution. He may even offer you "preferred" fees because of your previous relationship with the bank. He will appreciate an explanation from you about your new business and be flattered by your offer to keep him updated on new business developments.

In turn, you can be candid asking about such matters as banking fees, special services and future loan requests. If you sense a positive, mutually supportive attitude, you can probably stop looking for a business banker elsewhere.

If, on the other hand, you are in the position of beginning a relationship with a new bank, then an introduction (from a local businessperson or accountant or attorney) will give you greater credibility at the institution. A new banker — every banker, really — will appreciate current information about your business so that by the time you approach him for a loan, he will already "know" your business and be more inclined to approve a loan to a familiar face.

## Your Suppliers

In your own business, you will be concerned about being paid for services performed. So you can appreciate the concern a supplier might initially have about a new business customer — even if that customer is you.

Therefore, you will have to put yourself in his place. If he understands and believes your business plan, and believes you to be reliable and responsible, he may well offer you some credit. It may not be for the cost of an entire order, but even a partial deferral of payment due is helpful to a new business.

Suppliers are often prepared to act (in effect) as bankers, lending you their product or service rather than money. They expect you to live up to your understanding with them — and the consequences can be damaging to your future business-credit prospects if you don't.

As we note in Chapter 11, word-of-mouth can be a very helpful marketing technique — if it is favorable to you, your product or service. Conversely, word-of-mouth can be damaging if the words are of anger, disappointment or distrust. Therefore, be certain to honor and protect your relationships with your suppliers.

## Your Clients

Clients might appear to be an unlikely source of credit — and they are not really credit sources in the traditional sense. They are more accurately sources of accelerated cash flow — putting money in your hands sooner.

Often, a new consultant is so grateful for the order, for the client's business, that he is afraid to ask "for anything" from the client.

We are suggesting that you ask for something that is yours — or eventually will be yours — the money you will be receiving for performing your services. To a new business especially, *now* is the most important three-letter word in the dictionary.

To each of these groups — the banks, your supplers and your clients — the most important consideration in extending you credit is your reputation and your business conduct.

If you meet your obligations timely; report any unforseen problems to them without hesitation, and generally "take care of business" as promised, you will be in the most desirable category of all: *A business they want to do business with.*

# 15

# BECOMING YOUR OWN TIME AND MANAGEMENT CONSULTANT

It is possible for a consultant to store his knowledge — on a computer disk, in his mind, even on an index card.

It is not possible for a consultant to store his time. The ten seconds which just passed as you read the preceeding sentence can never be recovered.

For a consultant, the old saw that "time is money" is especially applicable.

Thus, you will have to budget and manage your time as if it were money.

## Regular Business Hours

When you worked in an office or at a plant, you were expected to report to work at a regular, established time each day.

You must expect no less of yourself when you are working on your own, especially if you are working at home.

You must establish — and adhere to — regular business hours.

This pattern will remind you each day that, at least during business hours, your home *is* your office, the place where you have elected to conduct your business. You must conduct your business in a business-like manner: *That productive attitude begins by maintaining regular business hours.*

## First, Set Goals

Long-range planning may be a desirable business school and corporate concept but it doesn't often work for the small business owner.

We suggest that you establish four reasonable categories of goals, of your reasonable business objectives:

**(1) What has to be done today.**

**(2) What has to be done tomorrow.**

**(3) What has to be done next week.**

**(4) What has to be done next month.**

## Next, Set Your Priorities

Not every goal or objective is equal. Therefore, you will have to establish some priorities.

If you are listing your goals on paper, highlight your priorities with a transparent marker so that they stand out from your less pressing tasks.

## Now, Keep Your Own Word

Your good intentions now have to be converted into action.

You must keep track of your objectives and priorities; they should be acted upon and reviewed during every working day. Two techniques should help you achieve them.

### (1) "Bunching"

Group similar tasks together. For example:

● Make all of your phone calls during a time set aside only for that task.

● Schedule out-of-office appointments with proximimty so that you can accomplish a series of visits on a single trip.

● Write or dictate all of your correspondence at the same time.

● Set aside a specific time for specific tasks, *e.g.,* billing.

This will save you time and mis-appropriation of energy.

"Bunching" will enable you to concentrate your energies on a related group of functions, increasing your productivity and safeguarding against deferring a given series of tasks "until later."

### (2) Become Your Own Management Consultant

Surprise — and test — yourself. Every so often, keep a very accurate daily log, or diary, of your activities. *Do not omit anything you do during the day — including drinking a cup of coffee, playing with the dog or doodling on your scratch pad.*

Then, at day's end, carefully review your activities.

Chances are your log will surprise you — and encourage

you to change (for the better) many aspects of the way you work. This is a wonderfully effective method of reviewing — and improving — your time-management habits.

# 16

# HOW TO WRITE A CONSULTING PROPOSAL

Some consulting clients, usually in private industry, are prepared to engage consultants on the basis of a conversation or a series of conversations. By simply talking out their problem and being impressed by the consultant's approach to solving it, they have developed sufficient confidence in his ability to help them.

Most consulting clients, including all government agencies, will not engage a consultant before receiving a proposal in writing.

In these instances, the quality and content of the proposal will determine which consultant will be given the pending assignment.

# What Should Be Included In A Consulting Proposal?

Four areas comprise the cornerstones of a successful consulting proposal.

### 1. Your Analysis And Definition Of The Problem

The prospective client has given you his version of his problem or project. Yet it is altogether possible that part of his problem is that he isn't entirely certain of exactly what his problem is.

You will have to define and analyze his problem in a clear and concise manner. He has to be completely confident that you, in fact, *do* understand his problem. If, by doing this in a skillful style, you provide him with greater insight, you will already be at an advantage by the time he has read this section of the proposal.

### 2. Your Approach To The Problem

New consultants, eager to acquire clients, have been known to provide solutions in this section of the proposal. Obviously, that can be a costly danger.

The function of this section is not to offer a solution, but to describe your approach to the problem. You will have to describe the steps which you will take towards reaching a solution.

Like all of the portions of the proposal, this section should be as clear and concise as possible. You can regard it the same way an architect regards a blueprint: This section presents your design of the assignment.

### 3. Your Qualifications For Being Given The Assignment

If the first two critical sections — your analysis of the problem and your design for solving it — are skillful, this section will simply support your worthiness to receive the assignment.

If the first two sections were just OK (but not unimpressive), then this section can renew your chances of winning the assignment.

In either event, the purpose of this section is to establish your qualifications for being awarded the assignment. It can include your educational background, your employment background and a list of references. It should be confident (but modest) so that the prospective client is convinced that you are the right consultant for this particular assignment.

**4. Your Summary Of The Consulting Assignment**

This is your last chance to win the assignment. Therefore, it should summarize your proposal as strongly as possible.

The only new element which should be introduced into this concluding portion of the proposal is a summary of the benefits which will flow to the client as a result of your successful solution.

Such a summary of benefits is often the key to being selected as the winner of a consulting competition.

# 17

# HOW TO MANAGE A CONSULTING ASSIGNMENT

Some consulting assignments will be performed on the client's premises. He may provide the consultant with an office and even a support staff for the duration of the assignment.

Most consulting assignments are performed outside of the client's plant or office.

In this more common instance, the consultant has to be aware of one problem which typically irritates consulting clients more than any other:

**The failure to stay in touch.**

It is true that the client has hired you to provide a solution, which will be the ultimate end product of your assignment, but he doesn't want to be left in the dark during the weeks or months it will take you to achieve that objection.

Thus, you have to be certain to maintain contact with the client throughout the consulting process.

A weekly phone call or a brief memo may be sufficient, depending on the nature of the client; but, no matter which communications system you employ, be sure to stay in touch with the client. That will serve as his "security blanket," his awareness that you are actively on his case."

The other mistake that new consultants are prone to make is to consider their final report precisely that. It is, in fact, just the beginning of a successful client/consultant relationship.

Your final report stays with your client long after your consulting assignment has ended. During the ordinary course of business, he will probably share it with others both inside and outside of his company. If he receives positive reactions during these moments, you will probably soon be receiving additional work.

One other thought: Several weeks after you have completed your assignment and delivered your final report, call the client to see if he needs any follow-up assistance from you. Perhaps he would like you to make a management presentation or to help his staff implement your conclusions. He may not require any additional input from you but he will long (and favorably) remember your spontaneous offer of service.

In a service business such as consulting, considerations such as these are both good manners *and* good business.

# 18

# HOW TO BECOME A ONE-PERSON "CONSULTING CONGLOMERATE"

A successful consulting practice can lead to an impressive number of ancillary "spin-off" business opportunities. Examples of such opportunities include:

**Seminars.** You can market your expertise by conducting seminars. Properly promoted, they can be very profitable.

**Speaking Engagements.** Corporations, government agencies and trade associations may invite you to speak at events on the basis of your consulting reputation. Such engagements can bring as much as $2500 per speech.

**Publishing.** An author's credentials can often make the difference between a published and an unpublished manuscript. If you have a book idea, your consulting credentials may be the key to winning a contract. Many consultants publish newsletters, as well. Successful newsletters can often provide income equal to or greater than the consulting business itself.

**Video and audiocassettes.** These are increasingly common profit centers for consultants. They can be sold by direct mail and even to clients who want to have them on hand in support of your other consulting services.

**Teaching.** Many community colleges and other institutions are adding specialized business courses to their catalogue of classes. If your specialty matches one of these offerings, you might be invited to join the part-time faculty. The title of "Adjunct Professor" can only enhance a consultant's credibility.

These possibilities are simply additional evidence that consulting is one of today's most rewarding self-employment opportunities.

If you are competent, confident and committed, then you can be the next person to achieve the success and satisfaction which so many consultant/entrepreneurs have already received.

# FOUR U.S. GOVERNMENT CONSULTING OPPORTUNITIES DIRECTORIES

Because it is so difficult to independently find the available consulting opportunities within the Federal Government, we have compiled this special section. It consists of four unique and useful directories:

(1) **35 Major Federal Civilian Purchasing Offices Which Buy Consultant Services**

(2) **The 12 General Services Administration (GSA) Business Service Centers**

(3) **Telephone Directory Of All 77 Small Business Information Offices**

(4) **Complete List Of All 33 Federal Offices of Small & Disadvantaged Business Utilization**

Each of these agencies — particularly the GSA — will be able to help you do business with the nation's biggest business of all.

# 35 MAJOR FEDERAL CIVILIAN PURCHASING OFFICES WHICH BUY CONSULTANT SERVICES

**1.** Agriculture Stabilization & Conservation Service, Man gement Services Division, Procurement & Contracting Branch, U.S. Department of Agriculture (USDA), Washington, DC 20250.

**2.** USDA Animal & Plant Health Inspection Service, Procurement & Engineering Branch, Federal Building, 6505 Belcrest Road, Hyattsville, MD 20782.

**3.** USDA Extension Service, Management Services Branch, Room 019 West Auditors Building, Washington, DC 20250.

**4.** USDA Federal Crop Insurance Corporation, Administrative Management Division, Administrative Services Branch, Washington, DC 20250.

**5.** USDA Food & Nutrition Service, Administrative Services Division, Procurement & Property Branch, 3101 Park Center Drive, Room 903, Alexandria, VA 22302.

**6.** Office of Procurement & Federal Assistance, U.S. Department of Commerce, Room 6855 HCHB, Washington, DC 20230.

**7.** Property & Supply Branch, Bureau of the Census, Federal Office Building No. 4 (Suitland), Room 1021, Washington, DC 20230.

**8.** Contracts Division, Logistics Service, Federal Aviation Administration (FAA), Washington, DC 20590.

**9.** FAA, Contracts Division, ALG-380, 800 Independence Avenue S.W., Washington, DC 20591.

**10.** FAA, Mike Monroney Aeronautical Center, AAC-70, Procurement Division, P.O.B. 20582, Oklahoma City, OK 73125.

**11.** FAA, FAA Technical Center, Contracts Services Branch, ACT-51, Atlantic City Airport, NJ 08405.

**12.** National Oceanic and Atmospheric Administration (NOAA), Chief, Acquisition and Grants Management Branch, AT/GMMI, 6010 Executive Boulevard, Rockville, MD 20852.

**13.** NOAA National Ocean Service Procurement Office, Atlantic Marine Center, 439 West York Street, Norfolk, VA 23510.

**14.** NOAA Environmental Research Laboratories, Procurement Division, National Bureau of Standards, 325 South Broadway, Boulder, CO 80202.

**15.** NOAA Environmental Data Service Regional Field Procurement Offices, National Climatic Center, Federal Building, Room 301-D, Asheville, NC 28801.

**16.** Office of Supply Services, Smithsonian Institution, 955 L'Enfant Plaza S.W., Suite 3120, Washington, DC 20530.

**17.** Department of Justice, Procurement & Contracts Staff, 10th & Constitution Avenue, N.W., Washington, DC 20530.

**18.** Immigration and Naturalization Service, U.S. Department of Justice, Contracting & Procurement Branch, 425 I Street, N.W., Room 2102, Washington, DC 20536.

**19.** Headquarters, National Aeronautics and Space Administration, Washington, DC 20546.

**20.** Contracting Officer, Bureau of Government Financial Operations, The Department of the Treasury, Madison Place

& Pennsylvania Avenue, N.W., Room 139, Washington, DC 20226.

**1.** Director, Office of Procurement Operations, U.S. Department of Energy, 1000 Independence Avenue S.W., Washington, DC 20585.

**2.** Division of Contract and Grant Operations, Office of Management Services, Office of the Secretary, Department of Health and Human Services, Room 443-H SP, 200 Independence Avenue, S.W., Washington, DC 20201.

**3.** Division of Contracting and Procurement, Social Security Administration, P.O. Box 7696, Baltimore, MD 21207.

**4.** Administrative Services Center, Public Health Service, 600 Fishers Lane, Room 3B-26, Rockville, MD 20857.

**5.** U.S. Government Printing Office, Materials Management Service, North Capitol & H Streets, N.W., Washington, DC 20401.

**6.** Division of Purchasing, Tennessee Valley Authority, Chattanooga, TN 37401.

**7.** Procurement Branch, Federal Communications Commission, Room 326, Brown Building, 1200 19th Street N.W., Washington, DC 20554.

**8.** Bureau of Reclamation, U.S. Department of the Interior, Washington Contracting Office, 18th & C Streets, N.W., Washington, DC 20240.

**9.** Bureau of Indian Affairs, U.S. Department of the Interior, Contracting and Grants Administration Office, Branch of General Service, 1951 Constitution Avenue N.W., Washington, DC 20240.

**0.** Bureau of Land Management, U.S. Department of the Interior, Administrative Services, 18th & C Streets N.W., Washington, DC 20240.

**31.** U.S. Fish and Wildlife Service, U.S. Department of the Interior, Division of Contracting and General Services, Branch of Contracts, 18th & C Streets N.W., Washington, DC 20240.

**32.** Procurement Office of the Office of Surface Mining, Division of Administrative Services, 1951 Constitution Avenue N.W., Washington, DC 20240.

**33.** Headquarters Contract Operations, U.S. Environmental Protection Agency, Washington, DC 20460.

**34.** U.S. Department of Labor, Office of Administrative Services, Division of Procurement, 200 Constitution Avenue N.W., Washington, DC 20210.

**35.** Small Business Administration, Office of External Awards, 1441 L Street N.W., Washington, DC 20416.

# THE 12 GSA
# BUSINESS SERVICE CENTERS

**District of Columbia and nearby**
**Maryland and Virginia**
7th and D Sts. SW., Room 1050
Washington, DC 20407
(202) 472-1804

**Connecticut, Maine, Massachusetts,**
**New Hampshire, Rhode Island, Vermont**
John W. McCormack Post Office and Courthouse
Boston, MA 02109
(617) 223-2868

**New Jersey, New York, Puerto Rico,**
**U.S. Virgin Islands**
26 Federal Plaza
New York, NY 10278
(212) 264-1234

**Delaware, Pennsylvania, Maryland,**
**Virginia, West Virginia**
9th and Market Sts., Room 5151
Philadelphia, PA 19107
(215) 597-9613

**Alabama, Florida, Georgia, Kentucky, Mississippi,**
**North Carolina, South Carolina, Tennessee**
Richard B. Russell Federal Bldg. and Courthouse
75 Spring St.
Atlanta, GA 30303
(404) 331-5103

**Illinois, Indiana, Michigan, Minnesota, Ohio, Wisconsin**
230 South Dearborn St.
Chicago, IL 60604
(312) 353-5383

**Iowa, Kansas, Missouri, Nebraska**
1500 East Bannister Rd.
Kansas City, MO 64131
(816) 926-7203

**Arkansas, Louisiana, New Mexico, Oklahoma, Texas**
819 Taylor St.
Fort Worth, TX 76102
(817) 334-3284

**Colorado, Montana, North Dakota, South Dakota, Utah, Wyoming**
Denver Federal Center
Bldg. 41
Denver, CO 80225
(303) 236-7409

**Hawaii; all of Nevada except Clark County; Northern California**
525 Market St.
San Francisco, CA 94105
(415) 974-9000

**Arizona; Los Angeles; Clark County, Nevada; Southern California**
300 North Los Angeles St.
Los Angeles, CA 90012
(213) 894-3210

**Alaska, Idaho, Oregon, Washington**
440 Federal Bldg.
915 Second Ave.
Seattle, WA 98174
(206) 442-5556

# TELEPHONE DIRECTORY OF ALL 77 SMALL BUSINESS INFORMATION OFFICES

## Alabama
Birmingham
(205) 254-1755
Mobile
(205) 690-2371
Montgomery
(205) 832-7310

## Arizona
Phoenix
(602) 261-3294
Tucson
(602) 792-6301

## California
Fresno
(209) 487-5069
Sacramento
(916) 440-3171
San Diego
(714) 293-6640

## Colorado
Colorado Springs
(303) 635-8911

## Connecticut
Hartford
(203) 244-3540

## Delaware
Wilmington
(302) 573-6364

## Florida
Jacksonville
(904) 791-2791
Miami
(305) 350-5751
Tampa
(813) 228-2351

## Georgia
Savannah
(912) 744-4208
Thomasville
(912) 226-2716

## Hawaii
Honolulu
(808) 546-7516

## Idaho
Boise
(208) 384-1242

## Illinois
Springfield
(217) 525-4270

## Indiana
Indianapolis
(317) 269-6234

## Iowa
Des Moines
(515) 284-4114

## Kansas
Topeka
(913) 295-2516

## Kentucky
Covington
(513) 684-1393

Louisville
(502) 582-6436

## Maine
Augusta
(207) 622-6171
Ext. 252

## Maryland
Baltimore
(301) 962-7611

## Massachusetts
Andover
(617) 681-5504

## Michigan
Detroit
(313) 226-4910

## Minnesota
St. Paul (Ft. Snelling)
(612) 725-4015

## Mississippi
Jackson
(601) 960-4449

Tupelo
(601) 842-0613

## Montana
Billings
(406) 449-5285

Helena
(406) 449-5285

Missoula
(406) 329-3117

## Nevada

Las Vegas
(702) 385-6444

Reno
(702) 784-5302

## New Hampshire

Manchester
(603) 666-7581

## New Jersey

Newark
(201) 645-2416

Trenton
(609) 989-2082

## New York

Albany
(518) 472-5447

Brooklyn (NYC)
(212) 330-7474

Buffalo
(716) 846-4588

Plattsburg
(518) 563-0860

Rochester
(716) 263-6288

Syracuse
(315) 423-5424

## North Carolina

Asheville
(704) 258-2850

Raleigh
(919) 755-4680

## North Dakota

Bismark
(701) 255-4011
Ext. 4316

Fargo
(701) 237-5771
Ext. 5453

## Ohio

Cincinnati
(513) 684-2306

Cleveland
(216) 522-4220

Columbus
(614) 469-6824

## Oregon

Eugene
(503) 687-6640

## Pennsylvania
Erie
(814) 452-2903
Harrisburg
(717) 782-4457
Pittsburgh
(412) 644-3340
Wilkes-Barre
(717) 826-6331

## Puerto Rico
Hato Rey
(809) 753-4370

## Rhode Island
Providence
(401) 528-4492

## South Caroliina
Columbia
(803) 765-5581

## South Dakota
Aberdeen
(605) 225-0250
Ext. 301
Pierre
(605) 224-5852

## Tennessee
Memphis
(901) 521-3675
Nashville
(615) 251-5221

## Utah
Ogden
(801) 625-6764

## Vermont
Burlington
(802) 951-6364

## Virginia
Charlottesville
(804) 296-5171
Norfolk
(804) 441-3330
Richmond
(804) 771-2101
Roanoke
(703) 442-8551

## Washington
Spokane
(509) 456-4663

**West Virginia**

Elkins
(304) 636-7405

Huntington
(304) 529-5555

Parkersburg
(304) 420-6034
Ext. 1276

**Wisconsin**

Milwaukee
(414) 291-3035

**Wyoming**

Casper/Mills
(307) 265-5550
Ext. 5427

Cheyenne
(307) 778-2220
Ext. 2341

# COMPLETE LIST OF ALL 33 FEDERAL OFFICES OF SMALL & DISADVANTAGED BUSINESS UTILIZATION

**Executive Office of the President**
Director, OSDBU
Washington, DC 20503
(202) 395-3314

**Department of Agriculture**
Director, OSDBU, Rm. 127 W
Washington, DC 20250
(202) 447-7117

**Department of Commerce**
Director, OSDBU, Rm. 6411
Washington, DC 20230
(202) 377-3387

**Department of Defense**
Director, OSDBU, Rm. 2A340
Washington, DC 20307
(202) 694-1151

**Defense Logistics Agency**
Director, OSDBU, Rm. 4B110
Alexandria, VA 22304-6100
(703) 274-6471

**Department of the Air Force**
Director, OSDBU, Rm. 4C255
Washington, DC 20330-5040
(202) 697-4126

**Department of the Army**
Director, OSDBU, Rm. 2A712
Washington, DC 20301
(202) 695-9800

**Department of the Navy**
Director, OSDBU, Rm. 604
Crystal Plaza, Bldg. 6
Washington, DC 20360
(202) 692-7122

**Department of Education**
Director, OSDBU, Rm. 2141
Washington, DC 20202
(202) 245-9582

**Department of Energy**
Director, OSDBU, Rm. 1E061
Washington, DC 20585
(202) 252-8201

**Department of Health and Human Services**
Director, OSDBU, Rm. 513D
Washington, DC 20201
(202) 245-7300

**Department of Housing and Urban Development**
Director, OSDBU, Rm. 10226
Washington, DC 20240
(202) 755-1428

**Department of the Interior**
Director, OSDBU, Rm. 2747
Washington, DC 20240
(202) 343-8493

**Department of Justice**
Director, OSDBU, Rm. 748,
HOLC Bldg.
Washington, DC 20530
(202) 724-6271

**Department of Labor**
Director, OSDBU, Rm. S1004
Washington, DC 20210
(202) 523-9148

**Department of State**
Director, OSDBU, Rm. 513 (SA-6)
Washington, DC 20520
(202) 235-9579

**Department of Transportation**
Director, OSDBU, Rm. 10222
Washington, DC 20590
(202) 426-1930

**Department of the Treasury**
Director, OSDBU, Rm. 127 W
Washington, DC 20250
(202) 447-7117

**Agency for International Development**
Director, OSDBU, Rm. 648 SA14
Rosslyn, VA 22209
(703) 235-1720

**Environmental Protection Agency**
Director, OSDBU, Rm. 1108,
CM No. 2 Code A149C
Washington, DC 20460
(202) 557-7777

**Export-Import Bank of the
United States**
Director, OSDBU, Rm. 1031
Washington, DC 20571
(202) 566-8111

**Federal Home Loan Bank Board**
Director, OSDBU, Rm. G-3, 4th Floor
Washington, DC 20552
(202) 377-6245

**Federal Trade Commission**
Director, OSDBU, Rm. 850
Washington, DC 20580
(202) 523-5552

**General Services Administration**
Director, OSDBU, Rm. 6017
Washington, DC 20405
(202) 566-1021

**National Aeronautics and Space Administration**
Director, OSDBU
Headquarters, Code K
Washington, DC 20504
(202) 453-2088

**National Credit Union Administration**
Directory OSDBU
1776 G St. NW, Rm. 6630
Washington, DC 20456
(202) 357-1025

**National Science Foundation**
Directory OSDBU
1800 G St. NW, Rm. 511A
Washington, DC 20550
(202) 357-5000

**Nuclear Regulatory Commission**
Directory OSDBU
Maryland National Bank Bldg.
Rm. 7217
Washington, DC 20555
(202) 492-4665

**Railroad Retirement Board**
Directory OSDBU
844 North Rush St., Rm. 1230
Chicago, IL 60611
(312) 751-4565

**Tennessee Valley Authority**
Directory OSDBU
1000 Commerce Union Bank Bldg.
Chattanooga, TN 37401
(615) 751-2624

**U.S. Information Agency**
Directory OSDBU
400 6th SW, Rm. 1719
Washington, DC 20457

**U.S. Postal Service**
Directory OSDBU
475 L'Enfant Plaza West, SW
Rm. 1340
Washington, DC 20260-6201
(202) 268-4633

**Veterans Administration**
Directory OSDBU
810 Vermont Ave. NW, Rm. 005C
Washington, DC 20420
(202) 376-6996

# ABOUT THE AUTHOR

Steve Kahn is an author, attorney and entrepreneur. As an entrepreneur, he has created new businesses in publishing, cable television and real estate. He has been the Executive Producer of "The Miss American Teen-Ager Pageant" for the ABC Television Network and a feature columnist for The New York Times Syndicate with a weekly audience of ten million Sunday newspaper readers. As an attorney, he served as Special Counsel and Director of Investor Relations for the Tishman Real Estate & Construction Co., Inc. He is the author of "THE SECURE EXECUTIVE: The Secret of Becoming One, Being One, Staying One." He holds a B.S. degree from New York University and a J.D. degree from New York Law School.

# ABOUT THE NO NONSENSE SUCCESS SERIES

More people than ever before are thinking about going into business for themselves — and the No Nonsense Success Guides have been created to provide useful information for this growing and ambitious audience. Look for these related No Nonsense Success Guides: *The Self-Employment Test* ... *Getting Into The Mail Order Business* . . . *How To Run A Business Out of Your Home* ... *How To Own and Operate A Franchise* . . . *How (and Where) To Get The Money To Get Started.*